CONTENTS

Spring

It is Spring at the seaside.

The tide is out on a bright sunny day. It is still too cold to swim.

A YEAR AT THE
Seaside

by Sally Hewitt
Photographs by Chris Fairclough

W
FRANKLIN WATTS
LONDON • SYDNEY

First published in 2004 by Franklin Watts
96 Leonard Street, London EC2A 4XD

Franklin Watts Australia
45-51 Huntley Street, Alexandria, NSW 2015

© Franklin Watts 2004

Editor: Kate Newport
Art director: Jonathan Hair
Photographer: Chris Fairclough
Designer: Steve Prosser

A CIP catalogue record for this book
is available from the British Library

ISBN 0 7496 4822 8

Printed in Malaysia

The tide comes in
and covers the sand.

You can crunch over the
pebbles and watch the waves.

A March wind
is blowing.

The sand is a good place
for flying a kite.

It is windy at sea too.

The fishermen wear
waterproofs to keep them
warm and dry.

Wooden breakwaters
protect the beach.

Tiny barnacles
cling to a post.

On the promenade, people enjoy the fresh Spring air.

Summer

When Summer comes,
children search for shrimps
and crabs in rock pools…

...and build sandcastles
before the tide comes in.

Sun cream protects
skin from the hot sun.

The Punch and Judy show makes everyone laugh.

You can swim in the
sea, or just sit and
enjoy the weather.

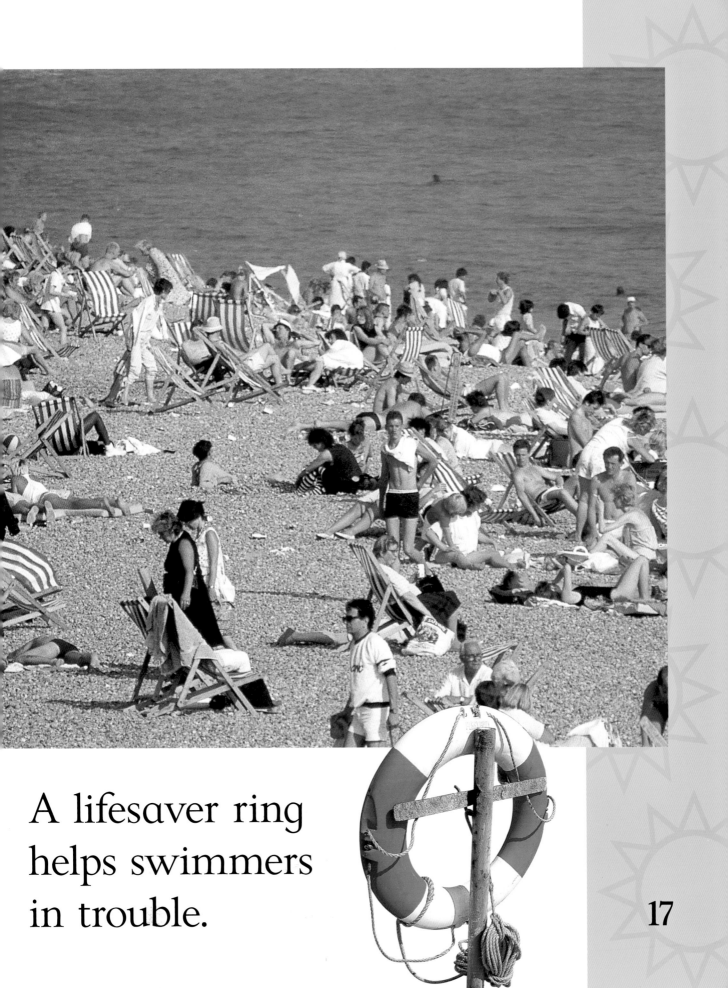

A lifesaver ring
helps swimmers
in trouble.

Autumn

In Autumn, most of the visitors go home.

Seagulls are hungry in the cold weather. There are fewer scraps for them to eat.

Rough waves splash onto the beach...

…and over the fishermen on the sea wall.

Now the beach is empty, horse riders can gallop along the sand.

The days become shorter
and the air is colder.

Winter

Beach huts are locked
up for the Winter.

People wrap up warmly
and walk along the shore.

Fishermen can paint their boats and mend their nets.

Sometimes, they bring their boats out of the water to do their work.

The pier is busy in all kinds of weather.

Don't miss the Christmas
show at the pier pavilion!

INDEX